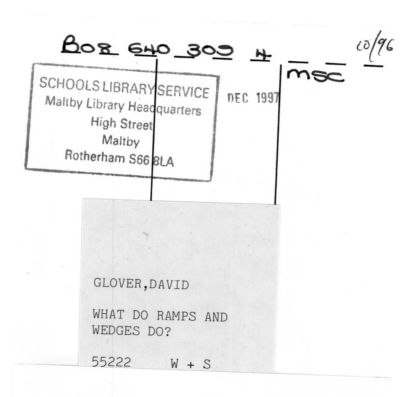

ROTHERHAM PUBLIC LIBRARIES

what do

Ramps and Wedges

do?

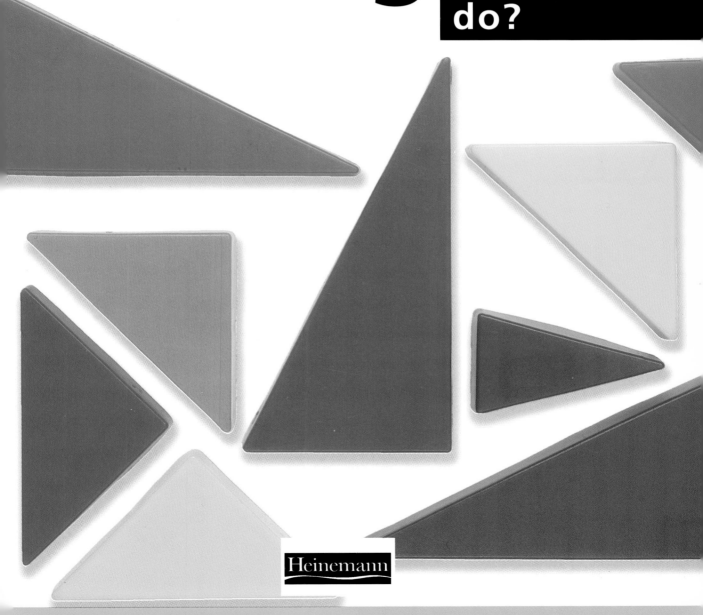

Heinemann

David Glover

First published in Great Britain by Heinemann Library
Halley Court, Jordan Hill, Oxford OX2 8EJ
a division of Reed Educational & Professional Publishing Ltd.

MELBOURNE AUCKLAND
FLORENCE PRAGUE MADRID ATHENS
SINGAPORE TOKYO SÃO PAULO
CHICAGO PORTSMOUTH NH MEXICO
IBADAN GABORONE JOHANNESBURG
KAMPALA NAIROBI

Designed by Celia Floyd and Sharon Rudd
Illustrated by Barry Atkinson (pp13, 14, 21) and Tony Kenyon (pp5, 6, 11)
Printed in the UK by Jarrold Book Printing Ltd., Thetford.

00 99 98 97 96
10 9 8 7 6 5 4 3 2 1
ISBN 0 431 06266 8

British Library Cataloguing in Publication Data
Glover, David
    What do ramps and wedges do?
    1. Inclined planes – Juvenile literature 2. Wedges – Juvenile literature
    I. Title II. Ramps and wedges
    621.8

Acknowledgements
The Publishers would like to thank the following for permission to reproduce photographs:
Trevor Clifford pp4, 5, 14, 15, 16, 20; Zefa pp7, 8, 12; Jess Stock/TSW p9; Sue Cunningham p11; J Ringland/TRIP p13; Leonard Lee Rue/Bruce Coleman Ltd p17; Colorsport pp10, 18, 19; Mary Evans Picture Library p22; Robin Smith/TSW p23.
Cover photograph by Trevor Clifford.
Commissioned photography arranged by Hilary Fletcher
Special thanks to Bobby and Rose who appear in the photographs.

Thanks to David Byrne for his comments on the initial draft.

The Publishers would like to thank Do It All Ltd and John Pollock The Ski Shop for the kind loan of equipment and material used in this book.

Every effort has been made to contact copyright holders of any material reproduced in this book. Any omissions will be rectified in subsequent printings if notice is given to the Publisher.

Contents

What are ramps and wedges?

A ramp is a slope for moving heavy things up and down. It is much easier to push something up a gentle ramp than up a steep one.

Less effort

When you push something along a ramp it goes up gradually. You use less *effort* than when you lift the load straight up into the air.

A wedge is a small ramp that you can move. It is easy to slide a wedge under a door. The wedge **jams** the door open with a large force.

Old and new ramps

How did the ancient Egyptians lift the stones to build the **pyramids**? They built ramps. Teams of workers dragged the huge stones up the ramps. They took the ramps away when a pyramid was finished.

Modern shopping centres have ramps for wheelchairs. People in wheelchairs cannot climb stairs. But they can go up and down a gentle ramp.

FACT

People power!

The Great Pyramids of Egypt are nearly 5000 years old. Every stone was moved by people or animals. In those days there were no bulldozers, trucks or cranes.

FILE

Zig-zags

It is hard work to climb a steep hill. You have to lift your body a long way with each step. A **zig-zag** path up a hillside takes you steadily to the top. You have to walk farther than if you go straight up, but each step is easier.

Skiers make zig-zag movements to come down a steep slope. If they skied straight down they would go too fast and might crash. The zig-zags help them to come down safely.

Hairpin bends

Roads zig-zag up steep hills so that cars can climb them more easily. The sharp bends between the zig-zags are called hairpin bends.

Blocks and chocks

Athletes use wedge-shaped blocks
at the start of a race. They are
called starting blocks, and they
help the runners to push themselves
off to a quick start.

This man is using metal wedges to split a block of stone. When he hammers the wedges into the stone, the wedge shape splits the stone apart.

Chocks away!

Chocks were placed under the wheels of aeroplanes. They are wedges which stopped the plane from moving until the pilot was ready. When he wanted to take off, he shouted 'Chocks away!'

Chocks away!

Axes and ploughs

An axe is a sharp metal wedge that is fixed to a handle. The handle lets you swing the axe head to hit a log with great force. The sharp wedge shape of the axe cuts into the wood and splits it apart.

The first axes

Simple stone axes were made by the first human beings hundreds of thousands of years ago. They tied wedge-shaped pieces of stone to wooden handles.

Farmers use **ploughs** to turn the soil. A plough has blades that cut into the soil. These blades are metal wedges. They make lines called **furrows**. This tractor is pulling a plough with several blades.

Knives and scissors

When you cut a carrot with a knife, the blade works as a wedge. The sharp edge of the blade is very very thin. It cuts easily into the carrot. The knife blade gets thicker away from the sharp edge. It forces the carrot apart.

Scissors are a pair of blades with sharp wedge-shaped edges. The blades work together to cut paper or cloth.

Secateurs are powerful scissors with a curved blade. They are used to cut twigs and branches.

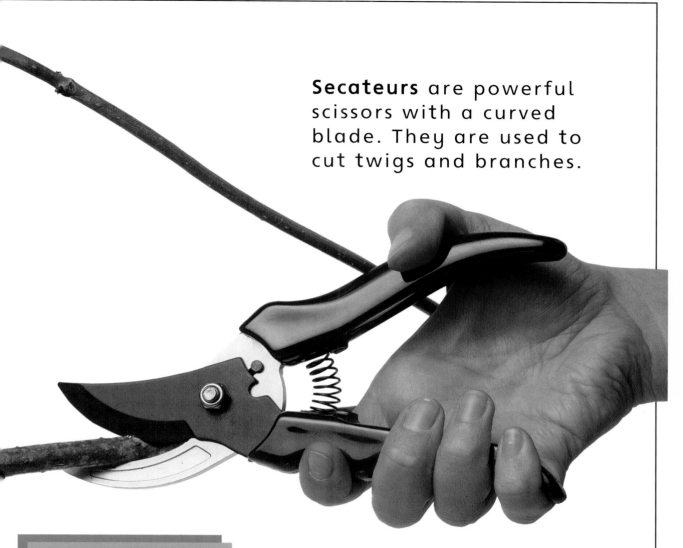

Teeth

Feel the shape of your front teeth.
They are wedges with sharp edges.
You use these teeth to cut and
bite your food. You
can feel how
they work
when you
take a
bite from
an apple.

Rats and mice have sharp incisor teeth for nibbling and gnawing their food. The beavers that live in North America can cut through tree trunks with their powerful wedge-shaped teeth. Beavers use the wood they cut to build their river homes.

FACT

Cutting teeth

The eight teeth at the front of your mouth are called incisors. The word 'incisor' means cutter.

FILE

Giant jumps

This water skier is jumping off a ramp. The skier comes up to the ramp at high speed. The slope of the ramp lifts her into the air.

This acrobatic skier is using a steep snow ramp to jump high into the air. He will be able to make amazing twists and turns before landing.

FACT

Ski jumps

An expert water skier can jump half the length of a football pitch.

FILE

Zip it up!

It is almost impossible to close a zip without the **slider**. Two wedges inside the slider press the teeth together when you zip it up. A third wedge pushes the teeth apart when you pull the slider down.

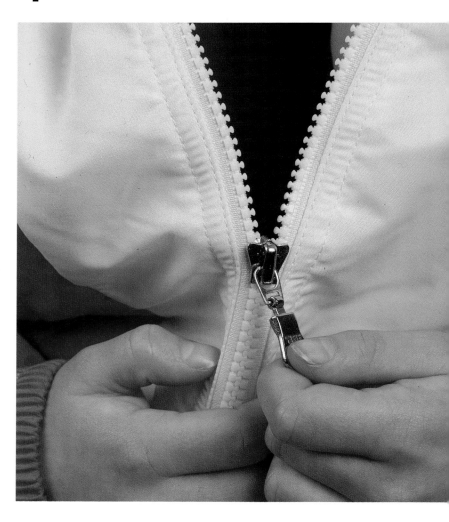

FACT

Zip invention

The zipper was invented in 1891 by an American called Whitcomb Judson. The first zips were used to fasten boots.

FILE

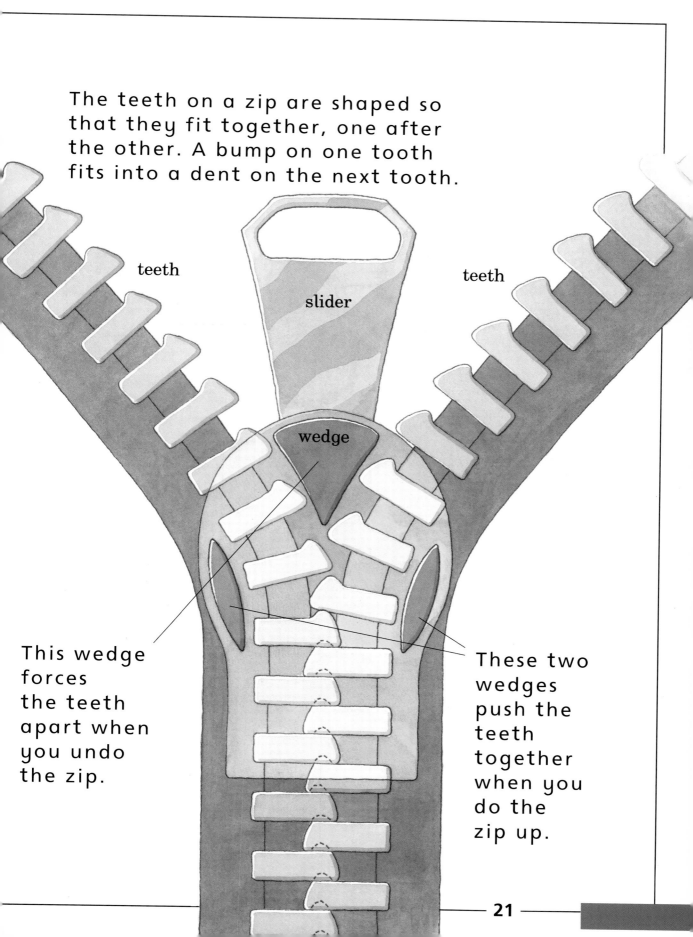

The teeth on a zip are shaped so that they fit together, one after the other. A bump on one tooth fits into a dent on the next tooth.

teeth

slider

teeth

wedge

This wedge forces the teeth apart when you undo the zip.

These two wedges push the teeth together when you do the zip up.

Slides and rides

Some of the most exciting fairground rides are slopes that you slide down at great speed.

Water splashes like this were popular 100 years ago. They are still great fun today. A rope pulls the car to the top of the slope and then lets the car go.

On the roller coaster your car
is pulled to the top of a steep
slope by a powerful engine.
Then you rush down the slope
on the other side. It is both
frightening and exciting at
the same time!

Glossary

chocks Wedge-shaped blocks for putting under wheels to stop them turning.

effort The pushing, pulling or turning force you must make to move something.

furrows The straight cuts or grooves in the ground that ploughs make as they turn the soil.

jam To block or wedge in one place.

motor The part of a machine that makes it go. Some motors are powered by electricity, others by petrol.

plough A machine with large blades pulled by a horse or a tractor. A farmer uses a plough to turn the soil in the fields.

pyramids Pointed mounds of stone. The ancient Egyptians built huge stone pyramids as places to bury their kings

secateurs Cutters which gardeners use to trim bushes and trees.

slider The part you move up and down to open and close a zip.

zig-zag A line that turns to and fro.

Index